Mamubah Derick Nforche

Sheep in the Midst of Wolves

AF190955

Mamubah Derick Nforche

Sheep in the Midst of Wolves

Wise as Serpent & Harmless as Dove

JustFiction Edition

Imprint

Any brand names and product names mentioned in this book are subject to trademark, brand or patent protection and are trademarks or registered trademarks of their respective holders. The use of brand names, product names, common names, trade names, product descriptions etc. even without a particular marking in this work is in no way to be construed to mean that such names may be regarded as unrestricted in respect of trademark and brand protection legislation and could thus be used by anyone.

Cover image: www.ingimage.com

Publisher:
JustFiction! Edition
is a trademark of
Dodo Books Indian Ocean Ltd. and OmniScriptum S.R.L publishing group

120 High Road, East Finchley, London, N2 9ED, United Kingdom
Str. Armeneasca 28/1, office 1, Chisinau MD-2012, Republic of Moldova, Europe
Printed at: see last page
ISBN: 978-620-0-10711-4

SHEEP IN THE MIDST OF WOLVES

You are surrounded by wolves, yet you must conquer and live as desired

> *Jesus knows the heart of people and what they are capable of doing. He knows that there are political wolves, financial wolves, religious wolves, academic wolves, wolves in business and technology etc. yet it did not discourage Him to tell His disciples "I send you as sheep in the midst of wolves".*

MAMUBAH DERICK NFORCHE

Table of Content

Introduction

INTRODUCTION

I am glad to come your way today and I have only one desire in my heart and it is to help you understand (as sheep) that living in this world as a morally upright and righteousness person is like walking on broken bottles. It is like running on smiling nails. Time and time again good people make the mistake of thinking that everyone else is like them and have the same heart that they have just to return with blisters and scars. They spread out their hands with the embracing heart of love just to return weeping and regretting. Majority of people out there are sharp thorns and at the slightest touch, they leave you bleeding. It doesn't take wolves long to injure their victim and the reason is simple. They see you as their prey and the needed food to satisfy their hunger and quench their thirst. That's how they survive.

Being naïve is a deliberate offer of yourself to be slaughtered on the altar of worldliness and that you have been a victim before does not hinder you from being a victim again. Man is constantly designing new weapons of mass destruction and new vocabulary to justify why they had to destroy. The truth is that you have a worldview and your worldview dictates your consecration and inspires your choices, your attitude toward people and things but what you don't know is that your worldview is unique to you alone. Others don't see this world and things (especially money and power) the same way you see them and so will not relate with people and things the same way you will.

To wholeheartedly throw yourself on people (even so called Christians) is a risk that you may not have the opportunity to relate your tale to willing and seeking listeners. Man has become a vicious thing and when they are biting you, they forget that the same blood flowing in them flows in you too.

To understand the gravity of the statement *"SHEEP IN THE MIDST OF WOLVES"*, examine the integrity of the one who made it – Jesus. The Bible is full of heroes and great personalities but from cover to cover, you will notice that only Jesus coined a phrase this beautiful to describe homosapien. This phrase alone tells us that humans are broken into two groups – sheep and wolves. If you are not one, then you are the other. There's no middle point with this. If you are not a sheep, then you are a wolf and all you need to proof who you are is to judge your own thoughts and examine your motives in the things that you do. A great writer (Zacharias Tanee Fomum) once made the contrasting statement "when God says 'I LOVE YOU' and the devil also says' I LOVE YOU', there's a difference". The words may be the same but one is coming from the Sheep and the other from the Wolf and they assuredly do not mean the same thing. Even if they said it so tenderly, if you are still logically thinking, you will know that one is seeking your good while the other is seeking your doom.

You cannot be half sheep and half wolf, the same way you cannot be half-light and half-darkness. You must distinctly choose and publicly declare to the world where you stand and stop fooling yourself and others who like you, think that there's a fence between the Sheep and the Wolf that you can sit on and be sheep today and wolf tomorrow. If any such fence exists, then it does only in your imagination. When God looks from on high, He knows which side you are in and when Satan is numbering his captives, he also knows which side you are in. You may want to dispute that it is possible to be sheep today and then be a wolf tomorrow but I need not be the one to respond to you because nature does. Has it ever been heard in history that a sheep born today becomes a wolf fifty years up the line and vice versa? Never! Let's give your claim a consideration. It is possible to be in God's camp today and tomorrow be in Satan's camp. In that case, a sheep has become a wolf. It is also possible to be in Satan's camp today and tomorrow be in God's camp. In that case, a wolf has become a sheep. What you should know is that this change is a one-time change. When a wolf becomes a sheep, he has become born again. When a sheep becomes a wolf, he has backslidden and become apostate. There's no fence on which you will sit and then God is holding your right hand on this side of the fence and the devil is holding your left hand on the other side such that you turn your head this way and discuss with God and in few minutes, your face is the other way discussing with the devil. God does not play such cheap game. He said "*if you are tired, then come (Mat. 11:28)*" and waits until you come by yourself. The prodigal son disappeared with his father's wealth and lived riotously. When he got tired, he arose and came back home. The father did not go around begging him to come back home.

To frequently fluctuate between sheep and wolf is an outcry beyond understanding. What it simply means is that you are still a wolf but intellectually and externally deceived that you are listed with the sheep.

This world is a battle ground between sheep and wolves and I want to tell us sincerely that wolves outnumber the sheep and are more vibrant, determined and strategic than the sheep. This is the reason why the sheep is a constant victim in the hands of these wolves. I seek to bring hope to the sheep. I seek to place before us victuals to enter this battle ground and return victorious. Look away from your scars. Smile at your chains because freedom has come. Point at your victimizer(s) and inwardly say "your time is up". May this little book become for the sheep a renewal of strength and an enlightening of the eyes of your heart in Jesus name? Amen

CHAPTER 1

BEHOLD, I SEND YOU FORTH

It is true that in John chapter ten, Jesus spoke of two types of sheep which we must look into to grasp wisdom for our own journey. He spoke of the "sheep that was already in the fold (v.1)" and the "sheep that was not yet in the fold (v.16)". The sheep that is in the fold hears His voice when He is calling and follows Him (v. 3-4). The sheep that is not yet in the fold have no idea who He is and cannot hear when He is calling even if He was calling them to escape a coming danger. In fact this sheep is still wondering in the wilderness of life and Jesus declared that they are just "another sheep not yet in the fold which He must bring in". These are those who are still wolves now but will someday willingly forsake their claim and become a tamed and admitted member into the sheep kingdom. Till then, they are still wolves and can still bite and damage their victims. They still have the venom of sin in their hearts and a heart that is not yet enlightened by the Gospel of Jesus Christ is capable of anything. Trusting a wolf is to deliberately use your life for experiment.

Behold, I send you forth as sheep in the midst of wolves: be ye therefore wise as serpents, and harmless as doves. 17 But beware of men: for they will deliver you up to the councils, and they will scourge you in their synagogues;

Matt. 10:16-17 KJV

See then that you walk circumspectly, not as fools but as wise, 16 redeeming the time, because the days are evil. Therefore do not be unwise, but understand what the will of the Lord is.

Eph. 5:15-17 NKJV

It is a worthy practice to always read things in their context because it helps to keep the discussion or debate within intended limits and saves the author from being accused of saying something that he did not say. Here, Jesus is saying *"behold, I send you forth as sheep in the midst of wolves"* and we must take this saying from Him seriously. One attribute of Jesus is that He does not say what He does not mean and does not teach what He does not practice. He is no careless speaker and all that He says is well calculated, divinely inspired and deeply meditated.

Jesus knows that the wolves are there but nevertheless He still sent them. He knew that wolves are not good to mingle with carelessly yet He did not wait for all the wolves to die before sending them. He added an emphasis in that phrase, a word often used to tell our audience to look careful and give us all their attention and concentration. He said *"Behold"* and then followed with *"I send you forth"*. Many may not want to go because of the wolves but Jesus looks at the wolves, their tendencies and still says to his disciples that *"I send you forth"*.

One of the most revealing verses in scripture that can help you fit your life into Divine context and gradually grow into giant-hood is *"As my Father hath sent me, even so send I you (John 20:21)"*. I know that you are a logical and intelligent thinker and so at this point I will like to make use of your thinking cap. What did Jesus mean when He declared to His disciples that He is sending them out in the same way that His Father sent Him? It could relate to circumstance and also to purpose i.e. the circumstance that made the Father to send Him and the thing He was sent to do. The Father sent Him to this earth to fulfill a particular purpose and thank God He did it and well. Now we are on stage and must do our part with the hope that we will also be faithful as He was. The other aspect to look at in His being sent by the Father is the "circumstance". How was this earth when He came? Was the earth filled with sheep or wolves?

It is certain that before He came, the earth was filled with wolves and so he came and lived in the midst of wolves. The same statement Christ made to His disciples *"behold, I send you forth as sheep in the midst of wolves"* is (I suppose) the same words that God spoke to Him too before He came to this world. He looked at Jesus and then turned and looked at the world and then told Him, *"Son! I am sending you to go and live in the midst of vicious men and women - wolves"*. God did not fear the battle but trusted the Son and the divine skills in him.

Anytime you read from anywhere or hear it coming from the pulpit that the righteous is as bold as a lion, don't look far to get understanding. God is the first being that this applies to and the second is Jesus Christ His Son who accepted the challenge to come and live amongst wolves. The third bold being is the "Holy Spirit". What He does is unbelievable. He is fearless and daring and when He undertakes a task, it must surrender no matter how strong it is. If you doubt me, go and ask Saul of Tarsus who became Paul the Apostle. If you are not very convinced, then go and ask Nebuchadnezzar to relate his tale with the animals and the empty throne that awaited his return from the forest – his quarantined home.

After this, then we follow the list of "the righteous as bold as a lion – Prov. 28:1" only because "greater is He that is in us than he that is in the world – 1 Jn. 4:4". Without Him INSIDE OF US, we are like vegetables. We fear the wolves but not Jesus. After working with His disciples for a while, he sent them out to confront the wolves. Wolves are to be confronted and not avoided and this is the eternal gap between the saints of today and the saints of old. We run away from battle but they were battle ready and could rise and enter the enemy's camp and force them to submission to the higher power. They started universities to fight the wolves and their philosophies. Today, we start universities to make money. They got involved in business to fight the wolves but today we get into business to live big. If you doubt me, go and read about John Knox, Martin Luther the Reformer, William Tyndale, Watchman Nee and so on. They traumatized the world of darkness in their time.

Intentionally, I did not mentioned saints in the Bible because I know that you see them as extraordinary human beings and some even believe that they did not exist for real. Since you doubt the accounts of scripture or have a mysterious way of seeing those saints, I decided to mention to your edification saints that lived few years back. They didn't fear the wolves but went after them. Sometimes these wolves were only human beings. At other times, the wolves were systems which could relate to politics, economics and human inequality. Read about Martin Luther Junior and Frederic Douglas and you will see men who brought systems down and won.

Today, the story is different. Saints who are the only soldiers the Lord has here on earth are more interested in money and living the "American dream" than their primary assignment. Every time you sit or stand, there are things you can see and others that you cannot see. You can see what is before (in front of) you easily than what is behind. If we use this to explain our attitude to money and material wealth, what should be before you should be your purpose and what should be behind you should be mammon and all that it brings. In Matthew chapter four, when Satan tried to bring it before Jesus, he did not only ask mammon and its glory to get behind him but added Satan to the things that should be behind him (Mat. 4:10). He only wanted to be seeing God before Him and Him alone all the time. If I could summarize for you the objective of Satan, I will simply say that he is constantly seeking to put certain things before you and make you focus on what should be behind you. He will put behind you what should be before you and before you what should be behind you. It takes one with the eyes of Jesus to know the difference and act adequately.

The society is terrible and no honest person will dispute it. What you don't know is that what is happening in this world is not a logical coincidence. Some people are creating all the mess and disasters that we are seeing and experiencing. They have their factories somewhere not too far from us. They spent much to build and equip it for the mass destruction of any area of the society they target.

True satisfaction can only be found in Christ Jesus. Outside of him, everything is slippery and will soon move from your hands to another's hands and then finally back to mother earth.

Jesus will not kill the wolves before sending you. He said *"behold, I am sending you forth as sheep in the midst of wolves"* and this should ring a bell in the heads of twenty-first century saints. You must still exist in the midst of the wolves and never become a wolf like them. You must leave the light beaming into their eyes that they someday bow helplessly seeking to be admitted into the sheep kingdom and are sincere about it. Stop running from battle because Jesus will look at you and say *"behold, I send you forth as sheep in the midst of wolves"*. Awake and face your destiny.

CHAPTER 2

SHEEP IN THE MIDST OF WOLVES

Haven convinced us that Jesus does not fear the decadence in this world and the presence of wolves, it is good to remind us again that He looked at his disciples and commanded them to "behold". To behold is to look critically and then understand. Simply put, it is to look, see and then hold. To hold is to grip and to grip is to possess and get the feeling of being in control and knowing what to do. When the teacher says "behold", he seeks to help you see beyond what the picture looks like. He wants you to see the main message being conveyed by that obvious picture. When you get the order "behold", know that your attention is being needed for something that cannot be seen or understood ordinarily. You have to avoid all forms of distractions before you can see what the teacher aims at conveying to your senses and once you get it, something happens to your imaginary world and fire drops in your bones. It affects your volition and may set you on fire that will need all the rivers in the world to quench. Why was Jesus so unquenchable? He was so unquenchable because He looked at the world, saw and understood. He knew how to mingle with wolves and come back as clean as He went out. This is why it is said *"he did not commit Himself to them because He knew their hearts – Jn. 2:24-25"*. Jesus is not a shadow boxer and if you are a student of His life, you will notice that every punch from Him always returned with the desired victory. Let the world become as dark as midnight, Jesus will still look at His disciples and say *"Behold, I send you forth"*. So, bid farewell to fear and hug your past failures for the last time because as you turn your back to them, it is now *"I perish, I perish"* because Jesus will still repeat to you "behold, I send you forth".

Behold, I send you forth as sheep in the midst of wolves: be ye therefore wise as serpents, and harmless as doves. 17 But beware of men: for they will deliver you up to the councils, and they will scourge you in their synagogues;

Matt. 10:16-17 KJV

See then that you walk circumspectly, not as fools but as wise, 16 redeeming the time, because the days are evil. Therefore do not be unwise, but understand what the will of the Lord is.

Eph. 5:15-17 NKJV

Jesus was an expert Rabbi and wise teacher who could communicate with everyone and they will understand if they were disposed by their heart conditions to. He used pictures or images to help people understand divine truths and realities. In this chapter, he looked at his disciples and said to them *"behold, I send you forth as sheep in the midst of wolves"*. He was not sending out sheep but human beings and they were not going to live amongst wolves but other human beings. He used "sheep" to describe those He was sending and "wolves" to describe those in whose midst they will live. Why did Jesus use "sheep" to describe those He is sending out and not "wolves"? I know your mind is not failing you and in the same direction as you, He did this to tell us that there are certain virtues that those going for Him must possess and the sheep embodies them. You cannot represent Him if you are a wolf.

Literally, a sheep is an animal and displays the unique virtues captured hence. Sheep is a meek animal. They are usually very quiet and gentle, holding themselves aloof from the world. In a herd, all the sheep tend to listen to their leaders and show esteem to them. Because of their obedient character, sheep are among the most popular animals beloved by mankind. This summary is so sweet that I feel like listing them separately for us to grasp and enjoy together.

The sheep is: -

- Meek animal

- Usually very quiet and gentle

- Holding themselves aloof from the world

- Listen to their leaders and show esteem to them

- Obedient character

Did you notice the phrase "because of their obedient character, sheep are amongst the most popular animals beloved by mankind?" Jesus will not send you out and then mankind will spit you out. The listed virtues indicates to you why those who claim to be sent by Jesus today have become a contradiction to the person of Jesus Himself.

If you are a student of Jesus's life, you will notice that all that is attributed to the personality of sheep above applies to Jesus. If you have studied the apostles and their work, you will also see a lot about the virtues listed for the sheep in their lives and ministry. The sheep is a meek animal. It is USUALLY very quiet and gentle. Jesus also said "I am meek and lowly – Mat. 11:28-30". Note the virtues – meek, very quiet, and gentle and find out if you have them or not. There are people that are not meek at all and claim to have been sent forth by Jesus. They are arrogant, proud and un-teachable and claim to have been sent forth by Jesus. There are people that cannot be quiet and listen. They are so noisy in speech and lifestyle. They are walking cymbals and are so pronounced for nothing. They may have the content and the grace but lack this great virtue of quietness. The sheep is not only quiet but very quiet. The apostles admonished Christians to be swift to listen and slow to speak and slow to wrath – James 1:19. Many people don't know how to lead a quiet life and mind their own business in this world. Many don't know how to focus and go unnoticed in this life. Merriam-Webster Dictionary says that to be quiet is to make very little noise and tending not to talk very much. Few people have this virtue my dear friend. I have often been humbled by the life of Jesus and I will share with you one of my discoveries. He never interrupted anyone that was talking to him. Even when the question was stupid and senseless, He will still listen quietly until the questioner comes to rest. Even when it is from the Pharisees, he will always patiently listen to them to the end. Whether the fellow was crying like Mary (the alabaster lady) or jubilating like Zacchaeus, He will still listen to them till the end. Whether it was the woman caught in adultery or the lawyer tempting him with his question of "who is my neighbor", He will still listen politely and never interrupted them. I find very few people with this virtue even when they are discussing on plain subjects. This disease is severe in those that have too much knowledge. Before you explain yourself, they already pretend to understand what you are trying to say and claim to have gotten to the end of your thoughts before you barely make the second sentence. It is true that some people are time killers and fun of repetition just saying the same thing in different ways. This type is sick too but my emphasis is on "slow to speak and swift to listen (James 1:19)" as a great attribute relating to the sheep.

It is also said of the sheep as always *"Holding themselves aloof from the world"*. They don't mingle with the world foolishly and I want to admit that few people understand what "the world" in this context refers to. It is not about mere humans but the formatting systems created to govern the activities of human beings. Many people just exist and do things because everyone else is doing them but turn mute when you ask them "why are you doing that"? It is a belittling reality that many people cannot explain why they do the things they do and stand firm on their point when you poke deeper on their convictions. The answers that I have often got is this "that's how everyone is doing it". They have no brains of their own and the work of thinking is relinquished to others on their behalf. The sheep hold themselves aloof from the world. The world will hardly toss them around because they master it and are bent to forever relate with it from that "aloof" standpoint. It is often said, eat with your enemy with a long spoon but this long spoon is more an internal thing than an outside one. It is an inner maturity beyond the enticing seductions of the outside. It is a mental freedom and a spiritual overtaking that the Christian has put Satan and his world behind him to have only God before Him – Mat. 4:10.

Another virtue of the sheep is that they *"Listen to their leaders and show esteem to them and have an obedient character."* These are outstanding attributes that are missing in many today. Jesus clearly said in John 10 that "my sheep hears my voice and follow me – v.4". This is a public declaration and global announcement that Jesus is the owner of the sheep and that the sheep belongs to Him. The emphasis "My Sheep" speaks louder than what we claim and we must drum this into every musical notes and frequency in our dealing with the sheep. If you claim to be the shepherd, then you must train yourself to recognize the reality that there's a Chief Shepherd that shall appear with His crown of glory to give those shepherds (stewards) who took great care of the sheep – 1 Pet. 5:4. Every shepherd (steward) has only one job and it is to connect the sheep to the chief shepherd so that they can hear His voice when He calls and follow Him. Anything less than this is weak and anything more than this is exaggeration and goes a long way to rather destroy and damage the sheep. You may not understand what you are doing until you stand before the chief Shepherd on that day. The sheep listen to their leaders and show esteem to them. They don't only listen to their leaders but also show esteem to them. They respect and honor and value them. They appreciate and obey them. Note that it is said that the sheep has "an obedient character." It is their nature to obey their master. They don't claim to know more than their master. They don't claim to suspect their master. They have a nature that willingly obeys their master once they hear his voice. They don't quarrel with obedience and this will justify why Jesus refers to those He send forth as "sheep". He will not send disobedient and independent people. He will not send people that when He calls, they will ignore and snob at Him. He sends them with clear instructions and expects that they will not modify it even if they are but a young and less experienced prophet standing before an older (more experienced) prophet – 1 Kings 13:11-31.

There's something called rebellion today and I wonder whether the apostles called it rebellion too. If the younger prophet had refused to bend to the direction of the older prophet, it would've been called rebellion today but was he really rebelling if he did that? I leave that to your discretion and whatever conclusion you reach, just ensure that you are in tune with the Holy Spirit and the eternal Word of the Most High God. God is the final authority and if you claim to be His sheep, then when you hear His voice, you MUST follow it.

WOLVES

Behold, I send you forth as sheep in the midst of wolves: be ye therefore wise as serpents, and harmless as doves. 17 But beware of men: for they will deliver you up to the councils, and they will scourge you in their synagogues;

Matt. 10:16-17 KJV

Jesus ensured that He told those that He was sending that He was sending them to live "in the midst of wolves." If you are a sheep in the fold of Jesus, then you must have a glimpse of your environment and the character of the people in whose midst you are living. They are wolves and wolves by nature are injurious and wild.

Wolves are the largest members of the dog family. Wolves can roam large and long distances, sometimes up to 12 miles (20 kilometers) in a single day. Wolves prefer to eat large animals like deer, elk, and moose. One wolf can eat 20 pounds (9 kilograms) of meat at a single sitting.

The wolf kills its prey by biting it in the neck area. It may also bite a large prey animal in the snout. The wolf might also bite smaller game, such as sheep, foxes and beavers, in the back. An animal killed by a wolf can have bite marks all over its body.

Wolves are out for serious business and hardly are they losers because they go out armed and prepared. They can roam kilometers in a single day and prefer to eat large animals. If they like large animals like deer, elk and moose, this mean that smaller game like sheep and foxes are nothing for them to destroy. If wolves are fearless before large animals like moose and elks, this should tell you a lot about the audacity of wolves. Not to make this chapter too long, I will fast forward to say that "an animal killed by a wolf can have bite marks all over its body." Sheep is a prey to the wolf and must understand that he is living in a society that can kill him at any time. The taunting question I keep asking myself is "why will Jesus boldly declare to his sheep that He is sending them as sheep in the midst of wolves?"

Many are happy with the Good Samaritan story. In that story, the robbers are the wolves and the man that fell into their hands was the sheep. By the time they were done with him, he had bite marks all over his body. After dealing with him thus, they departed living him half dead until the Good Samaritan came to that scene. The people out there are merciless and ungrateful in many ways. The wolf will always see the sheep as a prey i.e. something to feed on and they are many in the different works of life. They are in companies and they are at schools. They are in politics and they are in business. They are in science and they are on the pulpit as well. The wolves on the pulpit are not different from those in the nightclubs. They only have different postings and different job descriptions and are working for the same master – the dragon.

You will never leave the grip of wolves the same way you entered. Even if you escape, you will have to tell the story as a second chance given to you by destiny to warn others of your one time senselessness as I am doing now. So many people out there are bleeding because they once had to dine with a wolf. The havoc that political wolves have done to nations is beyond telling. Those in the entertainment can relate their own experiences of having to do with wolves. Those that came across pulpit wolves have a lot to say as well. The common denominator with all the wolf-victims in this world is the same – many bite marks all over their bodies. You cannot remain the same again – never. Your heart will be shattered and like the victim in the Good Samaritan story, you will be stripped naked and left half dead. Regardless of who you are, once in their grip, you are gone. Be you a genius, business tycoon, lay man, blind, deaf and dumb, once you've fallen into the hands of wolves, then you are in real trouble.

Jesus will not kill the wolves before sending the sheep but will send them nevertheless. The reason for sending them in the first place is to convert into sheep as many wolves that they can such that in the long run, the number in the sheep kingdom far outnumbers the one in the wolf kingdom. Who are those designing evil in this world? They are wolves and yet you are sent forth as sheep to live and influence in their midst. Praise the Lord for He is good and all the time.

CHAPTER 3

WALK CIRCUMSPECTLY

Haven gone as far as to let you know that Jesus is not ignorant of the fact that this world is full of wolves and that wolves are not friendly animals but fearless and vicious, He still went ahead to tell his disciples "behold, I send you forth as sheep in the midst of wolves". Knowing that as sheep in the midst of wolves, you are constantly dancing in the vicinity of danger and death, you must adopt a lifestyle that will guarantee your peace, safety and prosperity. There are wolves co-habiting the same neighborhood with you and there are wolves working in the same company with you. There are wolves attending the same lectures with you and there are wolves visiting the same markets with you. There are wolves in the same political party with you and there are wolves in the same church assembly as you. Suspecting people aimlessly is a bad habit but you must pick this one lesson from Paul which is in astounding agreement with what Jesus said. You must *"walk circumspectly and not as fools – Eph. 5:15"* and the reason is simple – *"because the days are evil v.16"*. Why are the days evil? *Because evil men and seducers shall wax worse and worse, deceiving many and being deceived themselves – 2 Tim. 3:13*. Those who are expecting that this world will become less wicked have not fully understood the mystery of the last days explained in scripture. If God does not help, even the very elect will be deceived. Those that are wicked today will be more intensely wicked tomorrow and the darkness today will become darker tomorrow. Once it concerns this world, there's no hope at all. They are on a jet speed towards eternal damnation and those who will remain faithful to the Son of Righteousness, the Man of Calvary, will attest to this claim someday. Reject it today and I agree with you. You have right to your opinion but hope that when it is time to accept the consequences of holding to your opinion and offering a deaf ear to this warning, you will not plead for a second chance and expect those you ridiculed years past to understand with you then.

Behold, I send you forth as sheep in the midst of wolves: be ye therefore wise as serpents, and harmless as doves. 17 But beware of men: for they will deliver you up to the councils, and they will scourge you in their synagogues;

Matt. 10:16-17 KJV

See then that you walk circumspectly, not as fools but as wise, 16 redeeming the time, because the days are evil. Therefore do not be unwise, but understand what the will of the Lord is.

Eph. 5:15-17 NKJV

From the pen of apostle Paul came one of the most beautiful and relevant phrases that one could table before humanity – *"See then that you walk circumspectly, not as fools but as wise"*. The first thing to do as sheep in the midst of wolves is to learn the art of walking circumspectly, without this, wolves will leave their many biting marks all over you as seen above. Take what you are about to read serious and arrange your life accordingly. What does it mean to walk circumspectly? By researching, I found out that to walk circumspectly is to be watchful and discreet; it is to be cautious and prudent. It also means to take heed, take action or make sure.

From Merriam-Webster Dictionary: -

Watchful

- Always watching the action of someone or something

- Not accustomed to sleep or rest

- Carefully observant or attentive

Discreet

- Not likely to be seen or noticed by many people

- Having or showing discernment or good judgment in conduct and especially in speech

- Unpretentious, modest

- Unnoticeable

Cautious

- Careful about avoiding danger or risk

- Marked by or given to caution

Prudent

- Having or showing careful good judgment

- Marked by wisdom

Take heed, Take action and Make sure

Merriam-Webster's Dictionary is helping us to understand what it means to walk circumspectly. I want you know that Apostle Paul was the one who churned out this counsel and if you know his story and journey very well, then you will understand the validity of this saying from him. He came into the fold late but before he died he claimed to Timothy to have fought a good fight - *"I fought a good fight and have finished my course, I have kept the faith – 2 Tim.4:7".*

This Paul went through a lot from the hands of wolves. He was constantly at loggerhead with these vampires and had a lot of marks on his body. So when he says, walk circumspectly, you better do well to heed to it. To walk circumspectly is to be watchful and to be watchful is to be always watching the actions of someone or something. You must ALWAYS be watching the actions of the wolves (someone) and their products (something). You must not be sleeping on the steering of your life. You must drive yourself to the desired destination with little or no blisters at all. We have to be fully awake and watching. Actions are manners, method of performing, attitude and gestures. What are the mannerisms of wolves? Many are acting blind all the time and are victims all the time. When I hear that a sheep is falling in love with a wolf and claiming that ""I will change him when I marry him" I just understand that such a sheep is acting blind to the mannerism, content and gestures of wolves, that's why preachers, writers and musicians are there. When the wolf will give you few bites and leave biting marks all over you, you will rush to either the preacher for counseling and prayers, a book for inspiration or musicians for solace.

Watchful

- Always watching the action of someone or something

- Not accustomed to sleep or rest

- Carefully observant or attentive

To be watchful is also referred to as "not accustomed to sleep and rest". This generation is not only sleeping but is deeply sleeping. This generation is in stupor and the future is fearful indeed. They are aware of nothing and are preparing against nothing. When one team does not show up for the match, the team that showed up wins by default and experts coin it to professionally standout as "default win". This is how the wolf wins all the time because the sheep is never showing up for the match. We are week, aware of nothing and preparing against nothing because of deep sleep. We are accustomed to physical and spiritual sleep. I know of a famous artist – Richard Bona who is faithful to his shows in the day and use his nights to work and produce songs. He stays up all night working and while others are sleeping, he is crafting his crafts. I talk about him because he publicly reveals his none attachment to any religious system but lives by two simple principles which are hard work and loving your neighbor as yourself.

While we are sleeping our destinies away, folks who understand this world and how wolves function, train their bodies not to be accustomed to sleep and rest. They work their way out of the rat race until they are above the basic rudiments of this world. It will not stop wondering me when I see Christians in deep and deadly slumbering. They claim to know their purpose in this world but use the day to glue to TV and social media and the nights to sleep and sometimes they sleep above eight (8) hours a day. You like sleep and rest and yet claim to be the disciple of one who only rested after He had completed the task that was attributed to His name – Gen. 2:1-2. Everywhere you go, when you hear my name remember that I am a crusader against LAZINESS AND EXCUSES and this is because I know the havoc it has done to Christians and to Africans. Continue to sleep dear watchman and the city will be invaded. Those who understand the concept of watchmen in the Old Testament will vividly understand what I am talking about. The city thrives because of the faithfulness and expertise of watchmen. Wake up and face your wolves.

To be watchful is to be "Carefully observant or attentive". You have to be observant and current with the activities of the wolf. You need to know what they are doing and see where they are going. You need to be able to look and plot a neat graph of their activities, decode their intention and decipher their victims. You must be attentive and your antenna must be apt to pick the frequency by which they are vibrating. You cannot be sleep-walking when you know that you have wolves in the same vicinity my dear friend. If you must sleep, go to a safe place and doze off. To be observant and attentive is to be analytical and for this, you need your brain and your inner eyes. The day you understand that you are in a battle and a battle you are expected to win, I can attest that your attitude will change.

Discreet

- Not likely to be seen or noticed by many people

- Having or showing discernment or good judgment in conduct and especially in speech

- Unpretentious, modest

- Unnoticeable

To walk circumspectly is to be discreet and to be discreet according to the dictionary is to live a simple life such that you are not easily seen or noticed by many people. There are many people that even when people don't see them, they do all to be seen and noticed. They constantly talk about themselves and their achievements. They constantly talk about their background, their achievements and their connections. They will always pull every discussion to point to something about themselves, what they had done in the past, what they are into now and what they plan to be in tomorrow. Their life is a noisy one. They are not discreet and so are not living circumspectly. They sound their own trumpet and make a lot of noise about who they are, where they are coming from and where they are going to. When you make yourself easily noticed, you multiply your problems and persecutions. Silent laborers are of more worth and strides than walking cymbals. How do you explain the fact that Jesus was quiet for 30 years even with all the wrong and injustice that was going on around Him? have you ever meditated on the fact that while Jesus was living in Israel, the Pharisees, Scribes, Sadducees, Herod, chief priests and the money changers were going on with their wickedness everywhere they were found? People were dying outside the will of God and going to hell but Jesus lived a discreet life and only came to stage when heaven approved it. Your controversies will be equal to the number of people you show yourself to because of your crave for recognition and appreciation. The wolves were there, yet Jesus lived a discreet life and when He came on stage, these wolves knew that someone braver than them is around and moved to the defensive side of the battle. They tried hard and finally crucified Him to their permanent undoing.

To live a discreet life is also referred to as having or showing discernment or good judgment in conduct and in speech. Note the words "to have discernment" and "to show discernment". You cannot "show" what you don't "have" and this is the mystified truth that many have refused to accept. When you apply pressure on toothpaste, what is inside will come out. This is the same with humans my dearly loved and precious friend and if I apply intense pressure on you, what you have inside will come out and who you are inside will show up. To "have discernment" is to smell from distance. It is to see danger way ahead before it reaches where you are so that you will escape before it reaches you. It is to smell the enemy's plans and comprehend their tactics while they are still plotting their attacks so that you can either flee or prepare an effective counter attack on them.

Discernment is a great virtue and I can tell you quite frankly that many people are void of it and you can see this by the way they cheaply get into troubles and "uncountable troubles" for that matter. After "having discernment", you must move a step further which attests that you will not be a victim in life. After having it, you must "show this discernment". What use will it be having discernment that you cannot show it? To show it is to let everyone see how through discernment, you are surviving all the attacks and traps of wolves. How can you have discernment that has grown to become "showing discernment" and be full of scars?

It is to "show good judgment" my dear brother and sister. I wonder if many understand what "good judgment" really is. It is that capacity to take a decision once and it was the best one. It is that potential that after proper analysis, your conclusion is the best one and when applied "blesses and adds no sorrow". You cannot have a good sense of judgment and make bad choices all the time. Whether your choice is related to marriage, business, number of kids to have, how to train them or where to build your house, if you have good judgment, you will hardly get into trouble. You will have a happy life because everything you do is well calculated and every harm and opposition clearly anticipated and planned for.

To be discreet is to be unpretentious and modest. If you are close to me, then you must be familiar with the phrase *"be yourself, heaven is not for perfect people; it is for honest people"*. This world is full of pretentious people seeking to make people see of them what they are not. In one word, this is hypocrisy and seeking the approval of men. This is the fastest way to enter the wolf's hands and they will teach you a lesson you will remember all your life. This is the fastest lane to losing self-confidence, self-worth and when you are no longer sure of yourself and depend on the opinion of others to thrive; you will become a victim life. To be an actor or actress is not easy at all but I keep wondering why you will leave God and seek to impress human beings. Find out how many ladies got abused by men simply because these men were appreciating and claimed to recognize their worth and value. Things as simple as appreciating their dressing, hairstyle, color choices, the way they walk, and eloquence will make them throw out their legs to one who is a stranger just to arise, cover their face with both hands and sprinkle crocodile tears on the ground. You don't claim to be wise with the wolf and you don't expect sympathy from him. When you are a pretentious person, seeking to be what you are not, your days are numbered and disgrace will come someday. Jesus hates hypocrisy and any good man or woman will hate it too. To walk circumspectly as Paul said, is to live a modest life. Be yourself and improve on your weaknesses as God gives you grace.

Cautious

- Careful about avoiding danger or risk

- Marked by or given to caution

The next thing about walking circumspectly is to be "cautious" and to be cautious" is to be careful about avoiding danger or risk. Proverbs says that a fool sees danger coming and walks right into it and this is the lot of many who don't walk circumspectly. Note that you cannot be cautious without having and showing of discernment as said above. It is discernment that makes you see the dangers and the risks ahead. Until you see them, you cannot avoid them. Until you see the plan of the wicked ones against you, you will not be cautious. What is interesting in this Merriam-Webster's definition is the emphasis that such a fellow is "*marked by or given to caution". His or her trademark is "cautious"*. It is a lifestyle and an obviously pronounced element in his life. It is a mark, a trait by which he is recognized. He is known that way and he lives that way. He is one given to caution and such people can only suffer one kind of problem in this life – persecution. I put this to you dear friends – what are you "marked by or given to" as you live in the midst of wolves? Are you always entering trouble? Are you always failing? Are you always getting entangled?

Prudent

- Having or showing careful good judgment

- Marked by wisdom

To be prudent is having or showing careful judgment. This, I have already spoken of above but so many are not prudent with their lives and opportunities. They are blind against tomorrow and live with no plan at all. The emphasis here is that a prudent person is one that is "marked by wisdom". In a spiritual sense, wisdom is Jesus but in general, it is "knowledge and experience". You have to be "marked by knowledge" and you also have to be "marked by experience". First you need knowledge but after you get it, you must go ahead to apply it and that's how you get experience. The greatest deficiency of the sheep today is "lack of knowledge". They don't want to know and so do not seek out knowledge. They don't want to be informed about life, this world, money, investments and so on. They have but one interest and it is to know the Bible and memorizing it well whereas their enemy the wolf lives outside the box. They are not marked by knowledge of life, purpose, humans, wolves, God, mercy, faith, grace etc. also; they are not marked by experiences – godly experiences. We are advised to "take heed", "take action" and "make sure" that we live circumspectly in this world because the days are evil. God is not asking your opinion whether you will like to walk circumspectly or not but said "make sure". This is a command from Him and His followers must heed to it.

CHAPTER 4

NOT AS FOOLS

This is interesting indeed that Paul tells them to walk circumspectly and not as fools. This informs us that there's a way fools walk and this should interest the sojourner whose interest is that after this toiling down here, should enter heaven finally and hear from his Maker the most beautiful phrase that the world eagerly seeks to here – "well done, good and faithful servant, enter rest".

Behold, I send you forth as sheep in the midst of wolves: be ye therefore wise as serpents, and harmless as doves. 17 But beware of men: for they will deliver you up to the councils, and they will scourge you in their synagogues;

Matt. 10:16-17 KJV

See then that you walk circumspectly, not as fools but as wise, 16 redeeming the time, because the days are evil. Therefore do not be unwise, but understand what the will of the Lord is.

Eph. 5:15-17 NKJV

Merriam-Webster's Dictionary says a fool is

- A person who lacks good sense or judgment

- A stupid or silly person

- A person lacking in judgment or prudence

The first thing to know is that a fool is a person and be sure that it is not you. A fool is someone who lacks good sense of judgment and the proof is that you are always getting into troubles and disappointments. You are always coming back to regret and weep alone. You can't be one who does a serious mental work and develop a thorough prayer life, analyze and interpret well and always get into troubles. When you do a thorough job, the conclusions you arrive at will not be problematic and every practical step you take paves the way for peace, spiritual and material prosperity for you. You may call it arrogance but the truth is that you sleep because you are a fool. You have all kinds of problems which are biting and frustrating your life. In the University of Problems, your name is present in every course of study. In the class of spiritual troubles, your name is present. In the class of emotional problems, you are present. In the class of poverty, there you go. In the class of ignorance, you are right in front. When you don't have a good sense of judgment, you will have an up and down life.

It is also said that a fool is a stupid and a silly person. Merriam-Webster Dictionary defines

Stupid as,

- Not intelligent: lacking or showing a lack of ability to learn and understand things

- Not sensible or logical

- Slow of mind

- Given to unintelligent decisions or acts

Silly as,

- Having or showing a lack of thought, understanding, or good judgment

- Not practical or sensible

- Not serious, meaningful, or important

A fool is one who is not intelligent. It is lacking and showing the inability to learn and understand things. It is not being sensible and logical. It is being slow of mind and given to unintelligent decisions and acts. So, when Paul was bidding them to walk "not as fools", he was urging them to develop the ability to learn and understand things in a sensible and logical way. He was urging them to have a mind that works fast and interpret issues and situations fast. Intellectually speaking, many people I know are mentally retarded and illogical thinkers. How do you explain that a person is falling at the same spot time and time again? You make a mistake and got fatally injured this year. Next year, you are making the same mistake thinking that the outcome will be different. Ladies make the same mistakes all the time and men do same as well. If you are praying for the same thing year after year, then you have a problem upstairs. Go to your dictionary and find out what "logic" is and then you will understand what it means to think logically. If your decisions are unintelligent as suggested by Merriam, tell me how your life will look like especially when you are living in the midst of wolves? You will be torn to pieces and at the end of your life when you look back to your history, you will bury your face in your hands and cry your eyes out. I don't need to be a prophet to tell you that because your life now is already telling you something in that light.

A fool is a silly person and being silly is having or showing a lack of though, understanding, or good judgment. It is not being practical and sensible. There are people like this. They are never practical in both discussion and application. They are always up to the task until you allow them to handle it and they mess up everything. Their mind and the way it functions is a complex equation that is never solving any problem. It is hard to understand why they behave the way they do and think the way they do. The shocking truth about the whole thing is when they too, cannot explain why they are the way they are and behave the way they do. Fools are crowd followers because they are not practical people. I have often asked people who are crying about one misfortune or the other how they plan to come out of their situation and they pin their gaze on me as if you were the newest art design of Michelangelo – that Italian Sculptor.

You have a problem that is killing you and have never sat to investigate the problem and beat it to submission. I don't think that being a spectator to life is the best side of the coin to choose because it will give you are frozen life and kill your mind. One of the words I have grown to hate is the word "impossible". What is impossible? What did you try? You have people who don't want to think and plan their future. They want you to do it for them while they remain glued on social media looking and commenting on others pictures and quotes. While they fancy with their days on earth, when they get jammed, they remember the house of the logical thinker and come panting with the expectation that you will think for them and understand how they got themselves embalmed like Lazarus before burial. When you kill your mind, you lose stability in life. A silly person is not serious and is not meaningful. When you look at what they are doing, you see no meaning in it and can predict a colossal end to it. Their ideas are not meaningful and their approaches are not meaningful either. Their choices are not meaningful and mirage is the seduction of their hearts and knowing what mirage is, chasing it or living for it is futility.

Scripture has a lot to say of fools. The fool says in his heart that there's no God (Psalms. 14:1). Who stand to lose when you make such assumptions - you or God? How will it help you if you convince your own heart that there's no God? This is the quest for freedom to live as you want with no guilt in your conscience. This is a deliberate desire to be a vagabond such that when you are rebelling against life and nature, even your own conscience will submit to your plight. Go into the sex industry and you will find many who stood aloof to this claim just to be on their knees in later years crying and weeping. Why do they weep later on? This is because seeking not to recognize the authority of God; they embraced a reprobate mind and became reprobate people. Find out what such a mind does in Romans 1. They have become experiments for vanity and any man or woman who pursues vanity becomes vain in life (2 Kings 17:15). There's no way out for that and when you take away the God concept from your mind, what is left is futility and you become a damaged person. You may have a great packaging but your content is gone. How can you look at nature and the way things happen and debate that God does not exist? Even if you don't want to give Jesus credit as supernatural, denying the existence of God damages you in many ways. Stand before the mirror and analyze the physiology of the man or woman you see in it and sincerely repeat to yourself that there's no God. Look at your eyes and how your balls fit the sockets and repeat your claim again. Look at your face and how the elements that make breathing possible are well organized and repeat your claim again. Imagine that everything else in you was right but you had no anus? So you mean to say you are a logical coincidence? A coincidence that is orderly is no coincidence at all. Every time you see order in anything, know that someone created that order. When I visit a home and find it neatly arranged and orderly, it will be mere stupidity to think that nobody did that job. When you dismiss the concept of God's existence from your heart, then you declare to nature that you are no longer interested in sanity and will become a specimen in the laboratory of the smart. What makes the sheep safe is his ability to recognize his master's voice and follow it and there's no way to follow a master you presume does not exist. We are all free to choose our lots in life but when the kickbacks start rolling in, be content with that too and don't look to the sky and expect He who does not exist to intervene.

My dear friends, even the prodigal son got to his wit end, recognized his father and shamefully came back home to accept the Father's love and mercy. Someday, you will realize that without Him in this life, you are a shattered person. I went that way also and know what it means to be nylon in the air on a windy day. The wind blows you to any direction it wants and you are just helplessly following.

It is a repeated claim that I love my life in Christ and not ready to sell it for anything my beloved friends. He said *"these things I have spoken unto you, that in me ye might have peace. In the world ye shall have tribulation: be of good cheer; I have overcome the world – John 16:33.* His peace I have found and can attest that it is nothing like the peace that the world gives (Jn. 14:27). With wolves in the same neighborhood that you live in, *"in this world ye shall have tribulations."* Few may understand this but let me summarize it for you with this quote from a great Christian thinker – *"I came to Christ because I needed something that I did not have and today I remain in Christ because I have something I will not trade – Ravi Zacharias".* How can I say in my heart that there's no God when I see His handwriting everywhere in nature. Look at the sun, the moon and the stars and be true to yourself. Look at the seasons, water, fetus in the womb, night, day, crops and so on and be honest with yourself. Even the free air you breathe should be telling you something about God and His generosity.

A lot is said of fools in scripture especially in the proverbs of Solomon and Ecclesiastes. Use a concordance and walk through all the verses referring to fools and you will be surprised to note that those you call fools (walking naked on your street and eating from trash) are not those that God call fools. You will be shocked that someone well dressed and speaking well can be a fool in God's eyes. Find out for yourself but don't be a fool in this world. Don't be stupid and silly in the midst of wolves because you will be harassed and badly injured.

CHAPTER 5

BUT AS WISE

Don't walk as a fool "but as wise" was Paul's admonition to the disciples in Ephesus. This admonition is relevant for us today as well. To be saved from wolves, you must walk as the wise do. It is to your own interest if you seek to know and comprehend the mannerisms of the wise. They hardly get into trouble because they are smart.

See then that you walk circumspectly, not as fools but as wise, 16 redeeming the time, because the days are evil. Therefore do not be unwise, but understand what the will of the Lord is.

Eph. 5:15-17 NKJV

See then that you walk circumspectly, not as fools BUT AS WISE. The word "then" in that phrase is very important my dear reader. It is important because it tells the fact that Paul is concluding on what he has been saying and is about to add one more advise. Paul was not talking to children in the above scripture; neither was he talking to young converts. He was talking to people whose faith in God was great, strong and vibrant. He was talking to people whose love for each other was fantastic (Eph. 1:15). To find Bible believing people today who love God passionately and one another in ways similar to David and Jonathan is not easy. It is possible but not easy. There's a popular phrase that each time I listen to it, it makes me laugh but it tells a vital truth about our generation. People often say that *"if you were very sick and traditional healers request that you bring a virgin as sacrifice for your healing, then you will just die"*. It is not true for there are still virgins out there but only in very insignificant number. These Ephesian brethren were wonderful people yet, to people with such understanding and spiritual balance, he said *"walk not as fools but as wise"* and prayed that the eyes of their hearts may be enlightened (v.18 NIV). This is interesting to you and me because if such people still needed the eyes of their hearts enlightened *"in order that you may know the hope to which He called you" v.18*, then we definitely need it more because of our spiritual tempo today.

Merriam- Webster Dictionary defines wise as

- Marked by deep understanding, keen discernment and capacity for sound judgment

- Aware of or informed about a particular matter

- Having or showing wisdom or knowledge usually from learning or experiencing many things

- Based on good reasoning or information

- Showing good sense or judgment

If we look at each of the above definitions and compare them with the way Jesus walked this earth, you will agree even if just reluctantly that Jesus was a wise man. His words and deeds were wielding wisdom at all time. No man or woman came to Him and left the same way. Some publicly exclaimed "where had this man this wisdom (Matt. 13:54; Mk 6:2)", this Man "increased in wisdom (Luke 2:52) and each time he uttered His thoughts, the audience melted unwittingly.

To be wise is to be marked my deep understanding but the question is "understanding of what"? Many well-meaning people particularly Christians have not taken time to brainstorm on this to their own detriment. To understand this is simple and we can get it. Let's look at Jesus and find out what He had understanding of. The truth is that Jesus did not only have deep understanding about God. He had deep understanding about God, life, human relations, nature, power, glory, fame, Satan, mammon, sin, demons, poverty, basic needs of life and what we should seek first. He knew about foundations, the laws of the land, the rulers and the priests. He knew about carpentry and many more. He was a Man deeply aware of many things and because of this intense knowing; it was very difficult to set him up. Before you came with you gimmicks like the lawyer in the Good Samaritan story (Luke 10), He could already understand what you are up to. He was smart because of the fact that He was marked by deep understanding. Why is it that many preachers brag about crowd today and Jesus did not? There's something He knows about crowd that preachers today don't know. Just read John 2:24 and you will see that He did not commit himself to them *"because he knew all men (KJV)"*. He knew that the same crowd singing "Hosanna to the son of David today will still say crucify him tomorrow (Matt. 21:9; 27:20-22)".

He was marked by keen discernment and capacity for good judgment. To discern is to detect with the eyes a figure or something that is approaching. Many only discover that they are already in a problem but the question is how did they get there without seeing it coming? The answer is simple – their discernment is not a keen one. They are impulsive folks and such will always run into problems whether they desired it or not. Jesus had many problems but they came as a result of persecution and because that was the only approved way to go about His plight. He saw the Father going that way (Jn. 5:19) and He could not go another way but apart from persecution, you could not get him into cheap trouble. He was wise with keen discernment and good sense of judgment. Many don't have a good sense of judgment because they have refused to develop their minds. When you don't know, you don't know and there's nothing apart from seeking to know and then study. No one was born with deep understanding on things. Those who know today know only because they invested to know.

The second suggestion of the dictionary on being wise stands out as being aware of or informed about a particular matter. How do you get informed on something? By reading about it and studying hard to gather and consume all that you can know about it. What is my pain and why do I bleed with all that is happening? I have said it before and will say it again. I am a crusader against Laziness and Excuses. You are not informed because you don't want to be informed and it is a shame today because the knowledge or information you need is just few clicks away at little or no cost at all. Have you heard of Wikipedia, Google, and YouTube before? They are free universities and you can access it from your bed.

It is also said of being wise as "having or showing wisdom or knowledge usually from learning or experiencing many things. Did you notice the word "learning" in that phrase? If you did and understand what it means, then I should stop pushing hard on this point. Now you know what to do. Go then and learn.

I have finally realized that poverty is a choice and not a heritage. We are poor because we don't want to know about riches and wealth. It is only when I started studying on wealth that I understood the outstanding difference between the poor and the rich. When you give money to the poor, they start spending and that's all they know how to do best - spend. When you give that same money to the rich, they first multiply it and only spend the interest of the interest of that money. That way, they are always having money but go back to the poor few months after and ask for that money again. It is long gone and that was me right there. Many Christians don't even know that this is a biblical principle and again I only understood it when I was seeking knowledge on the subject of wealth.

Do you remember the parable of the talents? He called in three servants and handed talents to each according to their capacities. He that received 5 produced 5 others. He that received 2 produced 2 more. He that received one went and buried it. Yet this third servant, I discovered is better than many of us today because when his master returned, he at least had what was given him to return to his master. During the time that the master was away, he was eating, paying his rents and yet still had the master's talent to return. The shameful truth is that if your master comes seeking for what He gave you, you will not even have it to give back to Him. Here, we agree that the guy who buried his talent is better than many of us today. When the master gave them the talents, they went on straight away to multiply it. God has been giving us money and the amount varies and comes in at different times. If you totalize it you will know your yearly income. Do you have this money to give back to Him if He comes seeking now? But why don't we know the art of multiplication of money? Why? This is because we are not interested in learning about it.

My latest discovery shook me from within and in a torturing way. What do we often call the basic needs of life?

- Food – what to eat

- Water – what to drink

- Rents – where to sleep

- clothes - what to wear

We call these things "BASIC NEEDS OF LIFE" and what you fail to see is the fact that if these things are referred to as BASIC needs of life, it means that life is worth more than these things. These are just basic and anyone living and toiling hard just to be able to have these things easily, is living a basic life because these things are the basic things of life. What it means is that you are not yet living the real life. You are only at the basic level even if these things are now readily available with no stress at all. If you rise in the morning running after these things and return in the evening seeking rest from these things, then you are at the basic level of life. I can tell you disappointingly that this is where many Christians are and don't even know it. They are still battling with the basic needs of life. They pray so much about it and hopefully gazing at the day when it shall be easy to get quality food, drink and designers dresses without much toiling. But this is basic life, not actual life yet and we are already contented. You are foolish because you want to be foolish. There are free books on any topic online if you are interested. Get them and feed your mind so that you can have deep understanding on things and keen discernment even about things that are still approaching. What you don't know, you don't know and if you do nothing about it, you will never know. Period!

CHAPTER 6

WISE AS SERPENTS

Jesus told His disciples that He is sending them to be in the midst of wolves but urged them to be wise as serpents.

Behold, I send you forth as sheep in the midst of wolves: be ye therefore wise as serpents, and harmless as doves. 17 But beware of men: for they will deliver you up to the councils, and they will scourge you in their synagogues;

Matt. 10:16-17 KJV

He did not just ask them to be wise but added the emphasis "as serpents" to His claim. They have a reference for the wisdom Jesus expects them to have. They should be wise as serpents. This takes us vividly to Eden where Eve had a taste of the serpent's wisdom. Jesus did not focus on the negative aspect of the serpent but told them to learn the wisdom of serpent. The serpent is cunny but cunningness is not what Jesus wants them to learn from the serpent. The serpent has venom and can kill but that's not what Jesus is magnifying for them to learn either. Jesus is picking a positive virtue from a negative character the same way you can get a lot of positive lessons from Goliath.

Snakes are wise because they calculate everything that they are doing and before you see them, they are done. They have no legs and so they coil around on the ground and on trees. They appear to remain on the same spot but with their persistent zigzag movement, they continue to move toward their target. Once they have seen their prey, they get to it without the prey noticing them. They are calculative and wise. From the story of the fall, you can see how the serpent put the whole world into the present predicament. He did not go to Adam but Eve. Why? The reason is obvious. He knew that he will easily convince her than the man. The woman represented a weakness in the man and so you don't attack the enemy where he is strongest. Study him well and then locate those two pillars that will bring down the whole building (referring to the death of Samson with the Philistines). The serpent is very strategic and you will discover why. He conceals his objectives and leaves you with just the result. The serpent will not come explaining or justifying, he operates and then disappears and you can only realize it when he is gone. Imagine that Adam and Eve fell without knowing that they had fallen. When they were realizing that they were naked, the serpent was long gone and tossing his victory wine. That's how smart this animal is and we ought to learn it. If you can stop talking about yourself and allow your results speak for you, it will make life more authentic for you and your activities. Stop blowing your own trumpet because in doing that you are alerting the enemies as well. Allow your victories to do that for you. While the results are making waves for the serpent, he is busy with the next thing in his plan.

The serpent is a good and sure communicator and once in discussion with him, he will get you if you are not smart and keen in discernment. You are in the midst of wolves and Jesus urges that you be as wise as a serpent. You should not be a careless talker because in much talking, the intents of the heart are revealed. They will decipher your burden and plot against of your journey and will put wolves along your way to hinder and destroy you. The serpent lives his results to speak for him. If they ask you how the world became so evil, you will not know what to say than to conclude that "it is the devil". The question is not who did it but how did he do it that no one noticed? Was it very obvious to the world that the devil was doing anything? In ways unnoticeable, he modified our banking system, our academic system, political system, entertainment, trade system and also technological system. He has wisely programmed the world my friend. He makes us all believe that it is technological advancement whereas he knows where he is going to. We are celebrating technological advancement while he is tossing his victory champagne for because he knows where he is going with this advancement. This is one of the wisdoms we should learn from the serpent and use against the wolves today. Get them engage on something else (i.e. purposeful distraction) while you are focusing on the main thing you want to achieve in life.

He has engaged us with something else so as to clear the way for the next thing in his plan. No one can explain how we gradually got here globally. Even our spiritual fathers did not see it coming because they are also victims in the devil's hands. He created a system that has squeezed them into his mold. Adam and Eve did not know what they were giving away. This again takes us back to the matter of having deep understanding. Adam did not have deep understanding about who he was and what God had put into his hands. The devil knew it and so when he was bargaining with Eve, he knew exactly what he wanted from them. When the devil is coming after you, he knows exactly what he wants from you. Unfortunately, many of us don't even know what we want in life. Eve was trying to defend what God had said without knowing it. The devil could easily see her loopholes and then capitalized on them.

You are a sheep by nature but you must be wise as serpent. Be a silent laborer and leave your results to speak for you. It is said of the spiritual man that he is like the wind and no man knows where he is coming from and where he is going to. This is one mark of spirituality that very few are accustomed to. Paul called it *"living a quiet life and minding your own business (1 Thess. 4:11 ISV)"*. This is all that the devil has been doing and succeeding very well - *living a quiet life and minding his business*. He is only minding his business and in a very salient way, has put the world under his captivity. The serpent doesn't make noise but has quietly turned the world upside down. This is the only way the sheep that is sent to live in the midst of wolves can survive and win. For us to turn the world upside down, we must learn this trick of the serpent.

When a thief is apprehended and is questioned after serious torturing, out of frustration, he says "it is the devil's work". I usually smile to myself because what he is saying is true but at that time, the devil has long gone and is popping champagne somewhere. Only his results speak for him. If you ask this unfortunate fellow to describe that devil he accused as being responsible for his acts, he will not even know where to start from. If you ask him to indicate where the devil is so that he should be arrested and prosecuted for instigating evil in the society, this man will not be able. That's how clean the devil operates. If only you could pick this lesson from him, this ability to effect change yet not known by anyone as responsible and it is your duty to find out how this can be done. You are making things to happen everywhere yet nobody knows who is at the origin of it all. You are overthrowing systems and remolding minds and preparing leaders for tomorrow in a very unperceivable way. Wow! This is the highest of it man and this is how the devil operates. The truth is that the devil does not create anything and even this wisdom of his, he learnt it from God. Because we have not been using it, it appears as though he authored it.

Isaiah said of God *"you are a God that hides yourself (Isa. 45:15)"* and the mystery of the Old Testament Temple speaks the same truth. The people knew Moses as their leader but that was not completely true. Moses only appeared to be their leader but their true leader was God Himself. Moses always went into the Holy of Holies (the Most Holy place) as the high priest to get instructions on what to do and for the people even when it had to do with sharing lands and inheritance to the people. When Moses is before God shaking and quaking, the people know nothing about that experience. They cannot even imagine what scrutiny Moses was going through but when he comes out, they bow to him in honor and reverence but Moses knows what he just went through in the hands of the true leader of the people.

So, God hid himself so much that the people believed in Moses as their true leader. God only came out when there was a fatal deviation from His standard or instituted authority. Sinai was God coming to correct a fatal problem. He is a God who hides Himself and very few people understand this concept. The Holy Spirit does the same thing. You can only see His works and sometimes you give credit to a man whereas the work was done by the Holy Spirit in the man.

The point is sufficiently emphasized and I have only one more idea to add. God created man and gave him authority over all the animals in Eden. How come man to whom all authourity was given fears some animals one of which is the serpent? You can see that the serpent imposed on man to fear and respect him. The serpent is supposed to run away from man (his boss) but now it is man (the boss) running away from the serpent (the slave).

The relationship between the sheep and the wolf is a scary one. The wolf is the boss and the sheep is its foe but one thing the sheep must do is to ensure that the wolf fear and respect him (Acts 5:12-13). It is possible but this will depend on the willingness of the sheep to impose his importance. Christians, including myself have relinquished our rights and moved to the backseat of history. We are nothing to reckon with in the society and even when we roar like lions, the noise we make does not go beyond our ceilings. Even in our roaring, there's fearfulness and ignorance. Be wise as the serpent and to recall it to you again, the serpent is an "unseen influencer". Only his results speak for him. You don't see him but you see his results. Secondly, he has imposed fear and respect of himself everywhere.

CHAPTER 7

HARMLESS AS DOVES

It is truly encouraging to see the chronology of the thoughts of Jesus from darkness to light. From something that does not make any sense to something that makes absolute sense. It didn't make any sense before when Jesus looked at His disciples and boldly told them "behold, I send you forth as sheep in the midst of wolves". It did look practicable but now, the full picture is registered in our minds and any sheep that really wants to, can live in the midst of wolves and be victorious. It is no longer a mystery because each segment of this verse is pregnant with success principles and if you follow them, you will live in the midst of the wolves in this world successfully.

Behold, I send you forth as sheep in the midst of wolves: be ye therefore wise as serpents, and harmless as doves. 17 But beware of men: for they will deliver you up to the councils, and they will scourge you in their synagogues;

Matt. 10:16-17 KJV

After admonishing them to be wise as serpent, He concludes that they should be "harmless as doves". Followers of Jesus who are harmful and injurious to other people are a disgrace to the kingdom of God. The son of righteousness was never here to condemn people but to save them. He came that all may have life and in abundance. He came that those who are heavy laden should find rest and those who take His yoke upon them will have peace in their souls. Jesus is a solution and not a problem. He does not solve one problem and create many. If anyone ever had a problem or accusing finger at Him, it was the world of darkness and the sons and daughters of the evil one and this will only be to the credit that he destroyed their falsehood. Why is Jesus angry with falsehood? This is because it destroys other lives and since he deeply values every life, he will not sit by and watch you make other human beings created in His image desecrated and abused so heartlessly.

He told them to be harmless as doves and I want you to know that to be harmless is to be one who is not causing harm to people and to things. To be harmless is to be one who is not dangerous and will not cause offenses. It is to be free from harm whether it is spiritual or physical harm. There are many in Christian setting that unknowingly entered the hands of religious wolves and today, they are formatted and pitiably brainwashed. It is sad to describe this but to see youths that are full of potentials, energy and reformative power wasting as they are today, is not easy to bare my dear friends. To see men who will be husbands and fathers tomorrow this destroyed make a seer sad because you can foretell what tomorrow will be like. I fear political wolves. I fear economic wolves. I fear educational wolves but of all these, I dread religious wolves the most. When you invoke the concept of the supernatural and use it to misguide people either willingly or unwillingly, that is terrible. They know that they are bowing to their marker but you are only squeezing substance from them. They open their lives to you in sincerity and trust but o! Little did they know that you were an injurious fellow and will make their lives more complicated and sad.

To be harmless according to Merriam-Webster Dictionary is to be "lacking the capacity or intent to injure". This is humbling and yet interesting at the same time. It is lacking the capacity to be injurious. This means that you don't even know how to be wicked and hurtful. The capacity is not in you and this was true of Jesus and is true of God. God cannot be wicked because there's no evil (darkness) in Him. It is not as if the capacity is there and then He is struggling with Himself not to be wicked. No! He doesn't have the capacity to be injurious.

The sheep cannot be injurious. The reason Jesus uses the image of "sheep" to describe His followers is not a mistake. It is a deliberate reminder of the way we are to live – as sheep. The sheep is harmless and if you claim to be a sheep and behave like a wolf, it means that resident in you is the capacity to be injurious. You have it inside and cannot be a trustworthy sheep.

Many out there are very careful with people who claim to be the sheep of Jesus Christ including me. I am very skeptical of all these pulpit gangsters and their followers and the reason is simple. I have been a victim in their hands. I awarded a contract to a so-called Christian Brother; tongue-talking and holy fire nonsense just to discover that I walked into the hands of a wolf. Looking gentle and looking spiritual but a wolf. My hard earned money went into his hands and he delivered to me a very bad product whereas I was going to him because I was avoiding wolves out there. Many ladies have been slayed by their spiritual fathers or brothers and many men have been slayed by their spiritual mothers or sisters. Sexually abused and financially robbed of their hard earned income. The truth remains that if you walk with your eyes closed today, you will get into trouble. I am a preacher, a brother but I don't take anybody who claims to be a Christian serious until I have passed you through what I call "The Integrity Test". Many fail this test without knowing that they have failed. When you bring money into the game, it helps you see the hearts of people. When you bring promotion into the game, you see people's true color. Dove is harmless. Dove is gentle and dove is clean. If you work on yourself to have these virtues (harmless, gentle and clean), and added to the previous chapters, I can attest that you will be an effective sheep and a successful sheep and God will set a table before you in the presence of your enemies.

In conclusion, Jesus will not kill the wolves before sending you. He is actually sending you to go and live in their midst and impose the values of His kingdom there. He has given us all the instructions needed to be successful in this journey. So, go and be wise as serpents. Go and be harmless as doves. Go and walk circumspectly. I wish you all the best.

MAMUBAH DERICK NFORCHE

Monday, 22nd, 2020